# The Renaissance

## A Rebirth of Culture

Stephanie Kuligowski, M.A.T.

## Publishing Credits

Dona Herweck Rice, *Editor-in-Chief*
Lee Aucoin, *Creative Director*
Torrey Maloof, *Editor*
Neri Garcia, *Senior Designer*
Stephanie Reid, *Photo Researcher*
Rachelle Cracchiolo, M.S.Ed., *Publisher*

## Image Credits

cover The Bridgeman Art Libary; p.1 The Bridgeman Art Library; p.4 Public Domain; p.5 (top) Alamy, p.5 (bottom) The Granger Collection, New York; p.6 The Granger Collection, New York; p.7 The Granger Collection, New York; p.8 Shutterstock, Inc.; p.9 North Wind Picture Archives; p.10 The Granger Collection; p.11 (top) The Granger Collection, p.11 (bottom) Public Domain; p.12 The Library of Congress; p.13 (top) The Library of Congress, p.13 (bottom) The Library of Congress; p.14 Bridgeman Art Library; p. 15 (top) The Granger Collection, p.15 (bottom) The Granger Collection;p.16 The Granger Collection; p.17 (top) Bridgeman Art Library, p.17 (bottom) The Granger Collection; p.18 (left) Shutterstock, Inc., p.18 (right) Shutterstock, Inc.; p.19 The Granger Collection; p.20 (top) Shutterstock, Inc.; p.20 (bottom) Shutterstock, Inc.; p.21 (top) Shutterstock, Inc.; p.21 (bottom) Shutterstock, Inc.; p.22 (top) Bridgeman Art Library, p.22 (bottom) Shutterstock, Inc.; p.23 Shutterstock, Inc.; p.24 Bridgeman Art Library; p.25 (top) Bridgeman Art Library, p.25 (bottom) Bridgeman Art Library; p.26 (left) Shutterstock, Inc.; p.26 (right) The Granger Collection; p.27 Getty Images; p.29 (top) Newscom, p.29 (bottom) Newscom; p.32 Shutterstock, Inc.; back cover Shutterstock, Inc.

---

**Teacher Created Materials**
5301 Oceanus Drive
Huntington Beach, CA 92649-1030
http://www.tcmpub.com

**ISBN 978-1-4333-5007-8**

Printed in China
Nordica.082019.CA21901024

# Table of Contents

# Cultural Rebirth

For nearly a thousand years, life in Europe changed very little. The Roman Catholic Church held most of the power. Rich landowners held vast estates. Poor farmers paid landlords a portion of their crops to live in simple shacks on the landlord's land.

Life was hard, and there was little time for studying, traveling, or having fun. People feared things they did not understand. To make matters worse, anyone who questioned the teachings of the Catholic Church could be punished.

*The School of Athens* by Raphael is one of the most famous paintings from the Renaissance.

Italian explorer Marco Polo leaves Italy for China.

In the late 1300s, change came first to Italy. When Europeans traveled to Asia, they discovered spices, silk, and perfumes. People in Europe wanted these items. Italy was located along the main trade route. As more goods came from Asia, more wealth flowed into Italian hands.

The **influx** of wealth meant that people had more free time and spending money. They read, studied, painted, sculpted, and played music. They questioned old ideas and made new discoveries. Western culture experienced a rebirth. The French call a rebirth a ***renaissance*** (reh-nuh-SAWNTS).

## Religion Matters

During the **Middle Ages**, the Catholic Church was a powerful force. The church taught that people should spend their lives earning a place in heaven. Scholarly work focused on religious questions. The art, music, and literature created during this time had religious themes. People worked hard to please God.

## Dangerous Times

Life in the Middle Ages was violent, with constant battles over land. Landlords, who had their own armies of knights, offered protection to the peasants. In return, the peasants worked the land and gave most of their crops to the landlords.

a knight

# The Renaissance World

## The New Middle Class

As Europeans began to venture farther from home, they discovered that the world had much to offer. New trade routes made it possible for them to travel through the Middle East to Asia. Travelers brought back exotic spices, silk, pearls, and perfumes.

Europeans were excited about the goods from the Far East, and they wanted more of them. Businessmen stepped in to fill the need. These businessmen, called ***merchants***, bought Asian goods and sold them in Europe.

merchants in Asia

Merchant ships arrive in an Italian harbor.

Merchants made a good living. They had free time and money to spend. They could buy the things they needed rather than making everything themselves. This created a need for workers to specialize in trades, such as weaving, glassmaking, and **carpentry**.

Many people quit farming to take advantage of the new opportunities in the trades. They moved to cities to find work as craftsmen and laborers. Cities grew quickly. A new middle class made up of merchants and craftsmen thrived, or succeeded, there.

During this time, all of Italy thrived. Its location between Western Europe and the Middle East made it the center of international commerce (KOM-ers), or business. Many of its cities, especially Florence and Venice, became rich and powerful.

## Adding Spice to Life

Today, it is hard to imagine people walking thousands of miles to buy cinnamon, cloves, ginger, or black pepper. But Europeans were thrilled by the discovery of spices. The new spices made food taste much better! This was especially true for meat. With no refrigeration, meat spoiled quickly. Spices helped hide the terrible taste of rotten meat.

## Banking Begins

Some merchants became so wealthy that they were able to loan money to others. They charged fees for this service. They often loaned money to kings and nobles. This led to the modern banking industry.

## Studying the Past

One man's love of books played a large part in starting the Renaissance. Francesco Petrarca (fran-CHES-koh peh-TRAHRK-uh), known as Petrarch (PEH-trahrk), was an Italian **scholar** in the 1300s. A scholar is someone who gains knowledge through learning and studying. Petrarch had a passion for the printed word. He searched Europe for texts written by ancient Greek and Roman scholars. He organized his books into a library and invited other scholars to study them.

Francesco Petrarca

Across Europe, many others began reading ancient texts. People found ideas that had been lost for a thousand years. They held the ancient Greek and Roman teachings in high regard. They also learned that these **translated** books contained many mistakes.

Translated books are books that are written by an author in one language and are then changed, or translated, into another language by someone else. People started to realize that they could not trust everything they read. So, scholars began to study the world for themselves. They performed experiments and made their own conclusions.

Italian scholars

## New Beliefs

Petrarch and the other great scholars of the Renaissance developed a new set of beliefs called ***humanism***. Humanism promoted the idea that every individual is important. It encouraged people to use their unique talents to create art, write poetry, and test theories. It wanted people to question long-held beliefs. Humanist ideas often went against the teachings of the Catholic Church.

## Spreading Knowledge

The city of Constantinople (kawn-stan-tuh-NO-puhl) fell to the Ottoman (OT-uh-muhn) Turks in 1453. The city's Greek scholars fled to the west and took ancient Greek texts with them. These texts gave Western scholars more material to study.

## Power Plays

In the 1300s, money was flowing into Europe along with imported goods. The merchants who bought and sold the goods were getting rich. **Monarchs** (MON-ahrks), or kings and other rulers, began collecting taxes on the merchants' earnings.

These taxes helped monarchs gain power. They used their new income to pay armies and to perform other government functions. They funded explorers' trips and artists' projects. They strengthened their power into central governments.

As the merchants and monarchs got more powerful, another group lost power. The landowners, who had ruled society during the Middle Ages, now had to answer to the monarchs.

In Italy, this shift of power took a different form. Italy was organized into about 250 **city-states**. Most city-states were like small countries and were ruled by groups of citizens. The men on these councils were rich merchants, craftsmen, and church officials. The ***signori*** (see-NYAW-ree), as these leaders were called, became more powerful than the nobility.

Merchants pay their taxes.

Groups of craftsmen, called ***guilds***, helped the signori hold onto their power. Each trade had its own guild. Guilds had rules for membership. In many areas, guild members were the only people who could vote and hold government offices.

A member of the weavers' guild gives his rules to the head of state.

Niccoló Machiavelli

## The Guild System

At one time, Rome had 55 guilds and Florence had 21. Florence's major guilds were lawyers, wool merchants, silk merchants, cloth merchants, bankers, doctors and apothecaries (uh-POTH-uh-ker-eez), craftsmen who used dyes, and craftsmen who used furs.

## Fearsome Rulers

The Italian rulers wanted to find the best ways to rule their city-states. They studied ideas about government. One popular theory was written by an Italian politician named Niccoló Machiavelli (ni-ko-LO mak-ee-uh-VEL-ee). In his book *The Prince*, Machiavelli advised rulers to take action that was effective, rather than morally correct. He taught that rulers should be feared, not adored, by their subjects.

## World Travelers

At the beginning of the 1400s, world geography was a mystery. On many maps, North and South America were nowhere to be found. The African continent trailed off in a chain of islands. Some maps even included sea monsters!

In 1453, the Ottoman Turks captured the city of Constantinople and marched into Europe. This military charge cut off Europe's trade routes to Asia. Merchants needed to find new ways to get their goods. This meant braving the unknowns of the open sea.

Vasco da Gama sets sail.

### Conquering for the Crown

In the 1500s, many Spanish explorers sailed west in search of gold and glory. To get what they wanted, they took native people as slaves, stole treasures, and burned everything in their paths. This earned them the name **conquistadors** (kawng-KEES-tuh-dawrs), or conquerors.

### Around the World in 1,095 Days

In 1519, a Portuguese sailor named Ferdinand Magellan (FUR-duh-nand muh-JEL-uhn) set out to sail around the globe. Five ships carrying 270 men left Spain with supplies for a two-year trip. Three years later, one ship returned with 18 survivors. Magellan died during the trip, but the expedition succeeded.

Columbus takes possession of San Salvador in the Bahamas.

Sailors from Portugal (PAWR-chuh-guhl) led the way. Prince Henry "the Navigator" mapped the west coast of Africa. Bartolomeu Dias (bar-TOH-lo-moh DEE-az) became the first European to sail around the tip of Africa in 1488. Vasco da Gama (VAHS-ko dah GAH-muh) sailed from Portugal to India in 1498. He returned home with a ship full of spices and a new water route to Asia.

Then, in 1492, an Italian sailor named Christopher Columbus took exploration in a different direction. He sailed west from Spain in hopes of reaching China. When he landed in the West Indies and South America, he believed he had reached the Far East. Columbus was mistaken, but he had opened exploration into "the New World."

Christopher Columbus

# The Art of the Renaissance

## Artists for Hire

In Renaissance Italy, merchants, guilds, and church leaders looked for ways to display their new wealth. They became **patrons** of the arts. As patrons, they hired artists to create works of art. These projects made the patrons, and their cities, look good.

Some of these works of art were portraits or statues of the patrons themselves. Others were public art projects that made cities more beautiful. And, many projects were done to glorify God or to bring honor to the Catholic Church.

Under this system, the arts thrived. Artists had countless opportunities to express their creativity. They earned good money. And, their positions in society improved. Patrons competed to attract the best artists to their projects. As a result, Italian cities are remarkable, even today, because of their many beautiful paintings, sculptures, and buildings.

Raphael's *Christ's Charge to St. Peter* was painted for Pope Leo X.

a painting of Lorenzo de' Medici

The Medici (MED-i-chee) family of Florence became famous for supporting the arts. The Medicis were wealthy merchants and bankers. Lorenzo de' Medici started a school for sculptors, where he discovered a teenage talent named Michelangelo (mee-kel-AHN-je-loh). Michelangelo went on to create some of the most famous works of art in the Western world.

## Magnificent Man

Lorenzo de' Medici, called Lorenzo the Magnificent, ruled Florence from 1469 to 1492. He was a wise man who wrote poetry, collected books, and surrounded himself with great thinkers and artists. He spent much of his family's wealth on art, including works by Botticelli (bot-i-CHEL-ee) and Leonardo da Vinci (lee-uh-NAHR-doh duh VIN-chee).

## A Powerful Patron

The Catholic Church was at the center of the patronage system. In fact, the church's spending on art put it deeply in debt. Raphael (rah-fahy-EL) was the favorite artist of Pope Leo X. Raphael painted for the Catholic Church his entire life.

Michelangelo

## Elisabetta Sirani

At a time when women had few opportunities, Elisabetta Sirani (ee-lis-uh-BET-tuh see-RAH-nee) rose to international fame as an artist. She began painting alongside her artist father at a young age. By 14, she was being paid for her work.

When Sirani's father got sick, the 17-year-old supported her family by painting. Many of her paintings featured strong women, including Mary, Judith, and Delilah (dih-LAHY-luh) from the Bible. She also painted Cleopatra, Portia (POHR-shuh), and her own self-portrait.

At age 27, Sirani died. Many believe the stress of supporting her family contributed to her early death.

*St. Jerome* by Elisabetta Sirani

## Advances in Art

The arts **flourished** during the Renaissance. Artists were in high demand. They were paid well and treated like celebrities. In this exciting climate, artists could try new techniques.

The growing use of oil paints in the early 1400s made it easier to experiment. The mixture of paint pigments and **linseed oil** made colors more vivid. Oil paint also dried more slowly than the paints of the past. Artists could take more time adding details.

Renaissance artists wanted to depict their subjects as realistically as possible. To do this, they studied the human body. They closely observed nature. This new realistic style was called ***naturalism***. One famous pioneer of naturalism was Donatello (daw-nuh-TEL-oh). He added lifelike details and human emotions to his sculptures that made them appear to be moving!

Donatello's *St. George*

This painting by Raphael shows a good example of perspective.

Another artistic advancement during the Renaissance was **perspective**. Perspective adds depth to paintings by making objects in the foreground larger than objects in the background. This is how the eye sees things. **Architect** Filippo Brunelleschi (fi-LEE-poh broo-nel-LES-kee) first mastered this technique. He used it in his architectural sketches. Painters soon began to use perspective in their work.

## Artistic Genius

Michelangelo grew up in Italy in the late 1400s. At age 13, he became an **apprentice** to a well-known artist. Within a year, he was being paid for his sculptures.

Lorenzo de' Medici, the ruler of Florence, recognized Michelangelo's talent. He invited the young man to attend his academy. There, Michelangelo studied the Medici collection of ancient Roman sculptures. This was a great opportunity for Michelangelo. He met many great humanists and future patrons.

In 1499, Michelangelo sculpted his first **masterpiece**—the *Pieta* (pee-ey-TAH). It is considered to be one of his greatest works. From a single block of marble, he carved two lifelike figures. With this work of art, Michelangelo became known as the most talented sculptor in Italy.

the *Pieta*

*David*

With the Catholic Church as his main patron, Michelangelo designed buildings, sculpted, and painted until the age of 89. His most famous works include the statue *David* and the **mural** on the ceiling of the Sistine (SIS-teen) Chapel.

Michelangelo had a thirst for knowledge and a passion for beauty. His work celebrated ancient history but used modern techniques. His life embodied the spirit of the Renaissance.

a small part of the Sistine Chapel ceiling

## Status vs. Passion

Michelangelo was born into a well-known family in Florence. At an early age, he had a passion for art, but his father tried to discourage it. His father thought art was beneath the family's social status. Eventually, Michelangelo's father helped him get the best apprenticeship in town.

## Student of Anatomy

Like other Renaissance artists, Michelangelo wanted to make his art more realistic. To learn more about human anatomy, he studied dead bodies at a hospital. He was curious about how the bones, tendons, and muscles worked together. This research helped him sculpt masterpieces like the statue *David*.

Andrea Palladio

## Classical Beauty

The Renaissance is best known for its painters and sculptors. Raphael, Botticelli, Michelangelo, and Leonardo da Vinci are just as famous today as they were in the past. But architects also flourished during the Renaissance. They created masterpieces on a grand scale.

Like other artists of the Renaissance, architects looked to the classical buildings of ancient Rome for inspiration. A trip to Rome to study the great buildings was part of every architect's training. They developed an interest in the symmetry, or balance, of the ancient Roman buildings. They also used Roman-style columns, arches, and domes in their own designs.

### Designing Homes

During the 1500s, merchants longed to escape crowded cities. They wanted to build restful country villas, or homes. Architect Andrea Palladio (puh-LAH-dee-oh) became an expert at designing elegant homes inspired by ancient Roman villas. Palladio's designs were later reproduced on English country estates and American plantations.

### Multi-Talented Men

Raphael and Michelangelo were famous painters, but both of these artists also worked as architects. In fact, they both worked on the design of Saint Peter's Basilica (buh-SIL-i-kuh) in Rome. The church is said to be the greatest architectural work of the Renaissance.

Saint Peter's Basilica

the Duomo in Florence, Italy

Filippo Brunelleschi is known as the first Renaissance architect. In 1420, he won a competition to redesign the dome of the Florence Cathedral, called the Duomo (DWOH-moh). He even designed cranes and other equipment to construct the dome. It is the largest brick dome ever built.

Leon Battista Alberti (LEE-on buh-TEE-stuh ahl-BER-tee) was another important architect of the Renaissance. Many of his designs were inspired by Roman temples. This is evident in the Tempio Malatestiano (TEM-pee-oh mah-lah-tes-tee-AH-noh) in Rimini (REE-mee-nee) and the Church of Santa Maria Novella in Florence.

Santa Maria Novella church

a Renaissance concert

## Shakespeare

William Shakespeare was an English playwright during the Renaissance. He wrote more than 35 plays and 154 poems. Shakespeare wrote many plays about Roman history. He also wrote many tragedies and comedies. He was part-owner of the popular Globe Theater in London, England, where many of his plays were first performed.

Shakespeare's plays are still performed around the world. His clever use of language and vivid imagery make him one of the most quoted people of all time.

a modern performance of one of Shakespeare's plays

## Popular Pastimes

During the Renaissance, the growing middle class had time to pass and money to spend. Music and theater became popular forms of entertainment. The Catholic Church and wealthy merchants paid musicians to write and perform music. As more time and money were spent on music, the art form evolved.

People began to write songs about topics other than religion. In Italy, a type of song called the ***frottola*** (FROH-toh-lah) became popular. This was a simple song with repetitive rhythms. Printers used the new printing press to print and sell sheet music of new songs.

**Madrigals** (MAH-dree-gahlz) first became popular in Italy in the 1520s. These were songs for two to eight people. They were often poems set to music.

At the same time, the violin, the **harpsichord**, and the **spinet piano** were invented in Italy. People bought these instruments to play at home.

Theater was another popular pastime. Playwrights wrote dramas and comedies based on ancient Greek and Roman tales. Theater companies built permanent theaters and charged admission. The average wage was one penny a day, but thousands of people regularly paid from one to 30 cents to see the latest play.

a Renaissance violin

Copernicus in the cathedral tower in Frombork, Poland, where he worked and studied

# Scientific Methods

The humanist scholars of the Renaissance filled libraries with classical texts. Artists, musicians, and writers found inspiration in these ancient works. But for science-minded scholars, the texts raised more questions than answers.

Humanists believed that all knowledge could be found in the ancient writings. They agreed with the classical scholars. They believed that logic alone could explain truths. But, some Renaissance scientists did not accept the theories they read. They wanted to observe nature and experiment for themselves.

In the early 1500s, Nicolaus Copernicus (NIH-koh-luhs koh-PUR-ni-kuhs) was one of the first scientists to try new methods. He built tools to observe the night sky. He observed, recorded data, and analyzed the data over many years. In this way, he realized that Earth revolved around the sun.

Copernicus's model of the universe

In 1605, Sir Francis Bacon developed the scientific method. Logic should be tested and retested with experiments, he said. Many scientists of the time agreed.

In the early 1600s, the telescope was a new tool for sailors. Italian scientist Galileo Galilei (gal-uh-LEY-oh gal-lee-LEY) built his own telescope to study the night sky. He was the first to see craters on the moon, Saturn's rings, and Jupiter's many moons. His careful observations proved many classical theories wrong.

## Controversial Ideas

Nicolaus Copernicus shocked the world with his new ideas. At that time, people believed Earth was the center of the universe. The Catholic Church supported this theory. They argued that God made human beings of supreme importance, so it was logical that they would occupy the center.

In 1543, Copernicus published his ideas in a book. The Catholic Church called him a **heretic** and put the book on the *Index of Forbidden Books*. Nearly a century later, Galileo proved Copernicus right. He, too, was called a heretic and forced to take back his ideas or be imprisoned.

Galileo explains his theories about the moon.

# Renaissance Man

No one embodied the spirit of the Renaissance better than Leonardo da Vinci. He was a painter, a musician, a scientist, an architect, and an inventor. He dedicated his life to satisfying his curiosity about the world.

Da Vinci was born in 1452 in a small town near Florence, Italy. When he was about 15, he became an apprentice to the best artist in Florence. Da Vinci's keen eye for detail and his ability to paint what he saw made him a star student.

Leonardo da Vinci

da Vinci's sketches of the muscles in the human arm

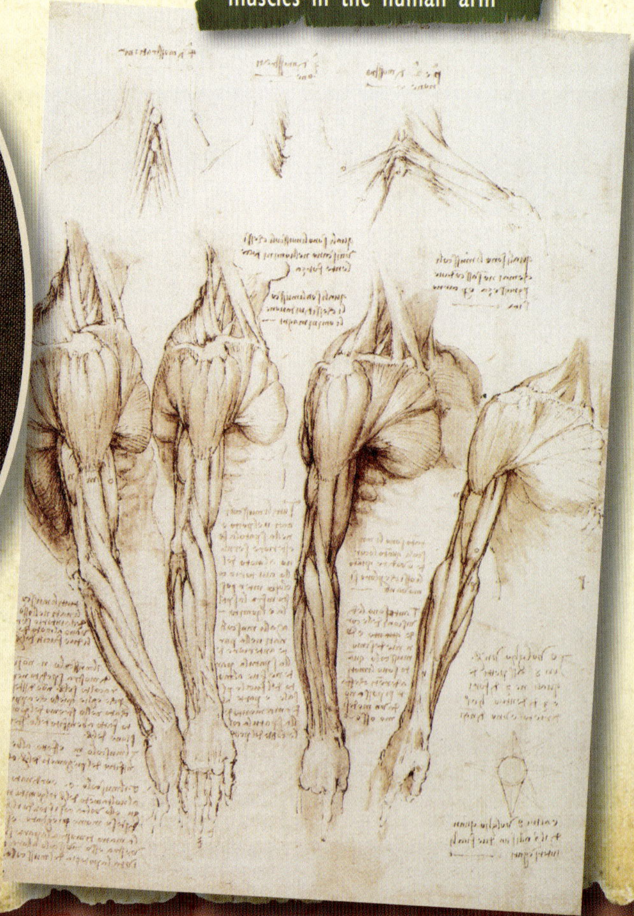

da Vinci's *Mona Lisa*

## Two Great Works

Leonardo da Vinci completed only a few paintings in his life. One of these is *The Last Supper*. Da Vinci used perspective to add depth to the painting. The facial expressions of the people in the painting are more lifelike than any other painting of the time.

Da Vinci's *Mona Lisa* is one of the world's most famous paintings. Many people today call it a perfect painting. The woman in the painting is famous for her mysterious smile. Her eyes seem to sparkle with life.

Even though da Vinci was trained as a painter, he followed his interest into the fields of music, science, and **engineering**. He was a court musician. He dissected corpses to understand the human body. He turned his careful studies of birds into flying machines. He painted two of the greatest artworks of all time. And, he designed machines and weapons for war.

Da Vinci was known as the greatest thinker of his time. Rulers paid him to live in their palaces because his presence made them look good. Today, da Vinci is thought of as one of the greatest thinkers of all time.

# Turning Point

The Renaissance was a time of cultural rebirth. Explorers traveled the world. They brought back new goods to trade. A middle class of merchants and craftspeople emerged. Members of this new middle class had more money and free time than ever before. They spent it on art, music, and theater. Artists now had many outlets for their talents. They tried new techniques and created masterpieces.

As the arts evolved, so too did technology and science. The printing press meant that books could be printed faster and cost less. This gave more people access to them. Scientists stopped trusting ancient theories to tell them how the world worked. Instead, they began observing and experimenting to learn things for themselves. They used the scientific method and new tools to study the world.

The people of the Renaissance saw the importance of the changes taking place around them. They wanted to create art, literature, and knowledge for future generations—and they succeeded. From the Renaissance, modern **Western civilization** was born. It was based on international trade, individual expression, and scientific inquiry.

the ceiling of the Sistine Chapel

## Lasting Legacy

Today, crowds flock to museums to gaze at the masterpieces of Renaissance artists. Renaissance buildings stand as monuments to the creativity and grandeur of the age. The poems and plays of Renaissance writers are regarded as some of the best literary pieces ever written. And modern-day scientists use the same methods of scientific inquiry developed by Renaissance scientists.

## Visiting the Renaissance

Many Renaissance masterpieces can be seen today in the Louvre (LOO-vruh) Museum in Paris, France. Da Vinci's *Mona Lisa* is one of the most popular attractions at the Louvre.

A crowd of people takes photos of the *Mona Lisa*.

# Glossary

**apprentice**—a person being trained by a skilled professional to do a trade

**architect**—a person who designs buildings

**carpentry**—the trade of a worker who builds or repairs wooden structures

**city-states**—self-governing states consisting of a city and surrounding territory

**conquistadors**—Spanish conquerors

**engineering**—the use of scientific and mathematical principles to design, manufacture, and operate machines

**flourished**—prospered, succeeded

**frottola**—a simple, nonreligious song that was popular in Renaissance Italy

**guilds**—groups of merchants or craftspeople who set trade standards

**harpsichord**—an early keyboard instrument similar to a piano

**heretic**—a person whose beliefs or ideas go against religious teachings

**humanism**—a philosophy that stressed the importance of individuals

**influx**—a flowing in of something

**linseed oil**—a yellowish oil made from flax seeds; used in paint varnish

**madrigals**—nonreligious songs sung by two to eight people in Renaissance Italy

**masterpiece**—an exceptional piece of creative work; sometimes refers to an artist's best work

**merchants**—people who buy and sell goods for profit

**Middle Ages**—the period of European history from about AD 500 to 1500

**monarchs**—people who rule by birthright, such as kings or queens

**mural**—a picture painted on a wall

**naturalism**—an artistic movement in which painters and sculptors tried to make their work more accurate and realistic

**patrons**—people who hire artists to create works of art

**perspective**—adding depth by making objects in the front larger than objects in the back

**renaissance**—French word meaning *rebirth*; a period of time in which European culture experienced a revival of art, science, and literature

**scholar**—a student or other highly educated person

**signori**—powerful leaders of the Italian city-states during the Renaissance

**spinet piano**—a small keyboard instrument similar to an upright piano

**translated**—text that has been reproduced in a different language

**Western civilization**—the way of life rooted in Greek and Roman culture and Christianity

# Index

# Your Turn!

In the 1400s, many Italians quit farming and moved to cities. These urban centers held promises of jobs in new trades. Cities were located along trade routes, so they were great places to see goods from foreign lands. They were also gathering places for great thinkers and artists. Florence was one such city.

## Making Plans

Imagine that you are a 14-year-old living in the Tuscan countryside in 1452. Your parents expect you to become a farmer, but you want to move to Florence to be a painter. Write a dialogue between you and your parents in which you discuss your future plans. Use what you know about Florence, the Renaissance, and the trade of painting to make a solid argument.